HOME-STYLE COOKING

Norma MacMillan

CAVENDISH HOUSE

Picture credits

Paul Bussell: 13.
Alan Duns: 5, 21, 25, 33, 37, 45, 57.
Don Last: 61.
David Meldrum: 53.
Roger Phillips: 9, 17, 41, 49, 61.

Edited by Isabel Moore

Published by
Marshall Cavendish Books Limited
58 Old Compton Street
London W1V 5PA

First printing 1981
Second printing 1983

Printed by L.E.G.O., Vicenza, Italy

ISBN 0 86307 095 7

CONTENTS

SOUPS

Philadelphia Pepper Pot

1 veal knuckle, sawn into 3 pieces
1 bouquet garni
6 peppercorns
5.1 litres/9 pints + 30 ml/2 tablespoons water
450 g/1 lb dressed tripe, cut into 2.5 cm/1 in pieces
1 onion, chopped
2 large carrots, peeled and chopped
2 celery sticks, chopped
2.5 ml/$\frac{1}{2}$ teaspoon red pepper flakes
2 medium potatoes, peeled and diced
30 ml/2 tablespoons cornflour
15 g/$\frac{1}{2}$ oz butter

1. Put the veal knuckle, bouquet garni and peppercorns in a very large saucepan and pour over the 5.1 litres/9 pints of water. Bring to the boil, skimming off any scum from the surface, then cover and simmer for 2$\frac{1}{2}$ hours.

2. Lift out the veal pieces and place them on a chopping board. Remove the meat from the bones and cut the meat into cubes.

3. Strain the stock and return it to the pan. Add the tripe, onion, carrots, celery, red pepper flakes, and salt and pepper to taste. Bring to the boil, cover and simmer for 1 hour.

4. Stir in the potatoes and veal cubes and simmer for a further 30 minutes or until the potatoes are tender.

5. Dissolve the cornflour in the remaining water and add to the soup with the butter. Stir until thickened, then serve hot.

Serves 6–8

4

Yankee Bean Soup

50 ml/2 fl oz oil
2 large onions, chopped
2 garlic cloves, crushed
6 tomatoes, skinned and chopped
4 celery sticks, chopped
225 g/8 oz dried red kidney beans, soaked overnight and drained
225 g/8 oz dried black beans, soaked overnight and drained
5 ml/1 teaspoon sugar
15 ml/1 tablespoon lemon juice
10 ml/2 teaspoons dried thyme
2.3 litres/4 pints beef stock

1. Heat the oil in a large saucepan. Add the onions and garlic and fry until softened.

2. Add the remaining ingredients with salt and pepper to taste and stir well. Bring to the boil, then cover and simmer for 3 hours.

3. Taste and adjust the seasoning before serving.

Serves 6

Cajun Gumbo

225 g/8 oz cooked ham, in one piece
1 garlic clove, crushed
4 onions, chopped
350 g/12 oz okra, sliced
700 g/1½ lb peeled shrimps
700 g/1½ lb tomatoes, skinned and chopped
175 g/6 oz tomato purée
750 ml/1¼ pints chicken stock
Tabasco sauce
1 green pepper, cored, seeded and chopped
450 g/1 lb cooked crabmeat, flaked
grated rind of 1 lemon
18 clams or mussels

1. Trim the fat from the ham and reserve. Cut the meat into cubes. Render the ham fat in a saucepan and pour off all but 30 ml/2 tablespoons. Reserve the remaining fat.

2. Add the garlic, onions, and okra to the pan and fry for 10 minutes. Stir in the shrimps and cook for a further 5 minutes. Remove the shrimps and okra from the pan and set aside.

3. Add the tomatoes to the pan with the tomato purée, stock, and several dashes of Tabasco sauce. Bring to the boil and simmer for 1½ hours. Stir in the ham cubes and okra and continue simmering for 30 minutes.

4. Heat the reserved ham fat in a frying pan. Add the green pepper and crabmeat and fry for 10 minutes, stirring frequently. Add to the tomato mixture in the saucepan, with the lemon rind and shrimps. Stir well.

5. Place the clams or mussels on top of the gumbo. Cover the pan tightly and steam until they open. Serve hot.

Serves 6–8

Manhattan Clam Chowder

125 g/4 oz diced salt pork
1 onion, chopped
4 large tomatoes, skinned and chopped
3 medium potatoes, peeled and diced
2.5 ml/½ teaspoon dried thyme
175 ml/6 fl oz tomato juice
600 ml/1 pint water
400 g/14 oz canned clams

1. Fry the salt pork in a saucepan until it has rendered its fat and the dice resemble croûtons. Remove from the pan and drain on paper towels.

2. Add the onion to the pan and fry in the pork fat until softened. Stir in the tomatoes, potatoes, thyme, and salt and pepper to taste.

3. Add the tomato juice, water, and juice from the canned clams. Bring to the boil, then cover and simmer for 12–15 minutes or until the potatoes are tender.

4. Stir in the clams and salt pork dice. Simmer for a further 5 minutes and serve hot.

Serves 6

(Top) Manhattan Clam Chowder
(Bottom) Pennsylvania Dutch Chicken Corn Soup

Pennsylvania Dutch Chicken Corn Soup

45 ml/3 tablespoons oil
2 onions, sliced
4 celery sticks, chopped
1.7 litres/3 pints chicken stock
10 peppercorns
125 g/4 oz egg noodles
450 g/1 lb chopped cooked chicken meat
450 g/1 lb canned sweetcorn kernels, drained
2.5 ml/½ teaspoon dried sage
1.25 ml/¼ teaspoon powdered saffron

1. Heat the oil in a saucepan. Add the onions and fry until softened. Stir in the celery and fry for a further 3 minutes.

2. Add the stock and peppercorns. Bring to the boil and simmer for 20 minutes.

3. Stir in the remaining ingredients with salt and pepper to taste. Simmer for a further 15–20 minutes or until the noodles are tender. Serve hot.

Serves 4–6

SEAFOOD

Baked Shad with Cornbread Stuffing

2 shad or herring fillets (about 450 g/1 lb)
75 g/3 oz butter
30 ml/2 tablespoons finely chopped spring onions
30 ml/2 tablespoons chopped green pepper
225 g/$\frac{1}{2}$ lb finely chopped mushrooms
40 g/1$\frac{1}{2}$ oz crumbled cornbread
50 g/2 oz crumbled water biscuits
5 ml/1 teaspoon dried dill
125 ml/4 fl oz water

1. Preheat the oven to 190°C/375°F (Gas 5). Lay the fish fillets in a lightly greased shallow ovenproof dish.

2. Melt 50 g/2 oz of the butter in a frying pan. Add the spring onions, green pepper and mushrooms and fry for 5 minutes. Stir in the cornbread and biscuits with the dill, and salt and pepper to taste.

3. Spread the cornbread mixture over the fish fillets, then fold them lengthways and tie in three places. Dot with the remaining butter and sprinkle with salt and pepper.

4. Pour the water into the ovenproof dish and cover loosely with foil. Bake for 30 minutes.

5. Remove the strings, cut the fillets in half and serve hot, garnished with lemon wedges.

Serves 4

Shrimp Creole

30 ml/2 tablespoons olive oil
2 large onions, finely chopped
1 garlic clove, crushed
250 ml/8 fl oz dry white wine
450 g/1 lb canned tomatoes, drained and chopped
15 ml/1 tablespoon red wine vinegar
15 ml/1 tablespoon sugar
1 large green pepper, cored, seeded and chopped
1 large red pepper, cored, seeded and chopped
15 ml/1 tablespoon cornflour
50 ml/2 fl oz water
700 g/1½ lb peeled shrimps

1. Heat the oil in a large frying pan. Add the onions and garlic and fry until they are softened. Stir in the wine. Bring to the boil and simmer for 10 minutes.

2. Add the tomatoes, vinegar, sugar, and salt to taste and mix well. Continue simmering for 10 minutes.

3. Stir in the peppers and simmer for a further 10 minutes.

4. Dissolve the cornflour in the water and add to the pan. Simmer, stirring, until thickened.

5. Stir in the shrimps and simmer for a final 5 minutes. Serve hot.

Serves 4

Shrimp Newburg

25 g/1 oz butter
225 g/8 oz peeled shrimps
50 ml/2 fl oz Madeira or sherry
2 egg yolks
450 ml/¾ pint cream
cayenne pepper
hot cooked rice or buttered toast
chopped chives or parsley to garnish

1. Melt the butter in a saucepan. Add the shrimps and cook gently for 5 minutes.

2. Stir in the Madeira or sherry and cook for a further 2 minutes.

3. Lightly beat the egg yolks with the cream. Add to the pan with salt and cayenne pepper to taste and cook gently, stirring, until the mixture is thickened and creamy.

4. Pour over hot cooked rice or buttered toast and sprinkle with chives or parsley.

Serves 2

Crab Louis

250 ml/8 fl oz mayonnaise
50 ml/2 fl oz double cream
50 ml/2 fl oz chilli sauce
50 g/2 oz chopped green pepper
30 ml/2 tablespoons finely chopped chives or spring onions
30 ml/2 tablespoons chopped stoned green olives
lemon juice
1 large lettuce, shredded
450 g/1 lb flaked cooked crabmeat

1. Mix together the mayonnaise, cream, chilli sauce, green pepper, chives or spring onions, and olives. Add salt and lemon juice to taste. Chill this dressing.

2. Arrange beds of shredded lettuce on four serving plates and pile the crabmeat on top. Chill.

3. Top the crabmeat with the dressing and serve.

Serves 4

Jambalaya

3 bacon rashers, rinded
1 onion, chopped
2 celery sticks, chopped
400 g/14 oz long-grain rice
600 ml/1 pint chicken stock
1.25 ml/¼ teaspoon cayenne pepper
1 bay leaf
1 large green pepper, cored, seeded and chopped
450 g/1 lb canned tomatoes, chopped with their juice
125 g/4 oz chopped cooked ham
225 g/8 oz chopped cooked chicken meat
225 g/8 oz peeled shrimps
chopped parsley to garnish

1. Fry the bacon in a saucepan until it is crisp and has rendered its fat. Remove the bacon from the pan and drain on paper towels. Crumble the bacon and reserve.

2. Add the onion to the pan and fry in the fat until softened. Stir in the celery and rice and cook, stirring, for 3 minutes. Add the stock, cayenne pepper, bay leaf, and salt and pepper to taste. Bring to the boil, then cover and simmer for 10 minutes.

3. Stir in the green pepper and tomatoes. Cover again and continue simmering for 5 minutes.

4. Add the ham, chicken, shrimps and crumbled bacon and stir well. Simmer, covered, for a further 5 minutes or until the rice is tender.

5. Discard the bay leaf. Serve hot, sprinkled with parsley.

Serves 4–6

MEAT

London Broil

---

4 × 225 g/½ lb rump steaks
Marinade
50 ml/2 fl oz white wine vinegar
50 ml/2 fl oz oil
1 garlic clove, crushed
15 ml/1 tablespoon lemon juice
4 peppercorns, coarsely crushed
5 ml/1 teaspoon salt

1. Mix together the marinade ingredients in a shallow dish. Add the steaks and turn to coat with the marinade. Marinate for 2 hours at room temperature, turning the steaks occasionally.

2. Preheat the grill. Drain the steaks and place them on the grill rack. Grill for 6–8 minutes on each side, depending on how well done you like your steaks. Serve hot.

Serves 4

Meat Loaf

700 g/1½ lb minced beef
350 g/12 oz minced veal
350 g/12 oz minced pork
4 slices of white bread
300 ml/½ pint milk
3 eggs
45 ml/3 tablespoons finely chopped celery
2 onions, finely chopped
30 ml/2 tablespoons chopped parsley
1.25 ml/¼ teaspoon dried thyme
1.25 ml/¼ teaspoon dried marjoram
1.25/¼ teaspoon dried basil
3 bacon rashers, rinded
125 ml/4 fl oz boiling water
50 ml/2 fl oz dry vermouth

1. Preheat the oven to 190°C/375°F (Gas 5). Put all the meat in a large mixing bowl. Tear the bread into small pieces and soak in the milk.

2. Add the eggs to the meat with the celery, onions, parsley, dried herbs, pepper to taste, and bread and milk mixture. Combine the ingredients thoroughly, using your fingers.

3. Shape the mixture into a loaf and place it in a buttered loaf tin. Lay the bacon rashers on top. Bake for 45 minutes or until the surface begins to brown.

4. Pour the boiling water over the meat loaf and continue baking for 45 minutes, basting once or twice with the vermouth and any juices that rise in the tin.

5. Unmould the loaf on to a warmed serving platter and serve hot.

Serves 4–6 with leftovers

Hamburgers

1.5 kg/3 lb minced beef
50 g/2 oz fresh breadcrumbs
5 ml/1 teaspoon dried thyme
1 egg, beaten
6 large hamburger buns, split

1. Preheat the grill. Mix together the beef, breadcrumbs, thyme, salt and pepper to taste, and the egg, using your fingers to combine the ingredients thoroughly.

2. Divide the mixture into six portions and shape into burgers.

3. Arrange the hamburgers on the grill rack and cook for 5–10 minutes on each side, depending on how well done you like your hamburgers.

4. Slide a hamburger into each bun and serve with sliced tomatoes, lettuce leaves, onion rings, ketchup and relishes.

Serves 6

New England Boiled Dinner

1 × 1.8 kg/4 lb salt brisket of beef
1 onion
1 bouquet garni
15 ml/1 tablespoon brown sugar
8 carrots, peeled
8 medium potatoes, peeled and quartered
6 small (button) onions, skinned
1 small cabbage, trimmed and cut into wedges

1. Place the beef in a large saucepan and cover with cold water. Bring to the boil, skimming off any scum that rises to the surface. When the scum stops rising, add the onion, bouquet garni and sugar. Half-cover and simmer for 2 hours.

2. Discard the onion and bouquet garni. Add the carrots, potatoes and small onions. Continue simmering for 30 minutes. Add the cabbage wedges and simmer for a further 15 minutes or until all the vegetables and the meat are cooked through.

3. Remove the beef from the pan and carve it into slices. Arrange on a platter and surround with the drained vegetables.

Serves 6–8

Red flannel hash : Leftover New England boiled dinner can be made into this classic. Mix together 450 g/1 lb of cooked beef, 4 cubed cooked potatoes, 225 g/8 oz cubed cooked beetroot and a chopped onion. Stir in 175 ml/6 fl oz of double cream, parsley, 5 ml/1 teaspoon of Worcestershire sauce, cayenne pepper to taste. Melt butter in a large frying pan, add the mixture and spread out evenly in the pan. Cook gently for 10 minutes, pressing down occasionally until a crust has formed on the base. Turn over and cook for 10 minutes or until a crust has formed. Serves 4.

Yankee Pot Roast

1 × 3 kg/6 lb topside of beef, boned and rolled
600 ml/1 pint red wine
1 onion, thinly sliced into rings
4 garlic cloves, peeled
7.5 ml/1½ teaspoons dried basil
25 g/1 oz butter
450 g/1 lb canned tomatoes, drained
50 g/2 oz stoned black olives
15 ml/1 tablespoon cornflour
30 ml/2 tablespoons water

1. Put the meat in a polythene bag. Add the wine, onion, garlic, and basil. Seal the bag and marinate in the refrigerator for 6 hours, turning the bag over occasionally.

2. Preheat the oven to 180°C/350°F (Gas 4). Remove the meat from the bag, reserving the marinade. Pat the meat dry with paper towels.

3. Melt the butter in a flameproof casserole. Put in the meat and brown on all sides. Pour in the reserved marinade and bring to the boil. Add salt and pepper to taste. Cover and place in the oven. Cook for 2 hours.

4. Add the tomatoes and continue cooking, covered, for 1 hour or until the meat is tender. Remove the meat from the casserole and carve it into thick slices. Arrange on a warmed serving platter and keep hot.

5. Strain the cooking liquid into a saucepan. Add the olives and bring to the boil.

6. Dissolve the cornflour in the water and add to the pan. Simmer, stirring, until thickened. Pour the gravy over the meat and garnish with parsley.

Serves 10

Broiled Pork Chops

1 large onion, thinly sliced into rings
6 thick pork chops
Sauce
50 ml/2 fl oz red wine vinegar
125 ml/4 fl oz tomato ketchup
10 ml/2 teaspoons sugar
2.5 ml/½ teaspoon ground cloves
5 ml/1 teaspoon celery seed
2.5 ml/½ teaspoon mustard powder
1 bay leaf

1. Preheat the oven to 180°C/350°F (Gas 4). Spread the onion rings over the bottom of a greased shallow ovenproof dish that is large enough to hold the chops in one layer. Rub the chops with salt and pepper and place them in the dish.

2. Mix together all the ingredients for the sauce and pour over the chops.

3. Bake for 1 hour or until the chops are cooked through and tender. Discard the bay leaf before serving.

Serves 6

Baked Spareribs

25 g/1 oz bacon dripping or butter
1 onion, chopped
30 ml/2 tablespoons vinegar
30 ml/2 tablespoons sugar
50 ml/2 fl oz lemon juice
250 ml/8 fl oz tomato ketchup
45 ml/3 tablespoons Worcestershire sauce
10 ml/2 teaspoons strong mustard
125 ml/4 fl oz water
5 ml/1 teaspoon dried basil
15 ml/1 tablespoon chilli powder (optional)
30 ml/2 tablespoons chopped parsley
1.8 kg/4 lb American-cut pork spareribs

1. Preheat the oven to 230°C/450°F (Gas 8). Melt the bacon dripping or butter in a saucepan. Add the onion and fry until softened. Stir in the vinegar, sugar, lemon juice, ketchup, Worcestershire sauce, mustard, water, basil, chilli powder, if used, and parsley. Bring to the boil and simmer for 30 minutes.

2. Meanwhile, sprinkle the ribs with salt and pepper and arrange them on a rack in a roasting tin. Bake for 30 minutes. Drain the fat from the roasting tin. Remove the rack and place the ribs in the tin. Brush them with the cooked sauce.

3. Reduce the oven temperature to 150°C/300°F (Gas 2) and bake the ribs for a further 1½ hours, brushing them frequently with the sauce.

Serves 4

CHICKEN

Creamed Chicken Livers

---

50 g/2 oz butter
2 onions, thinly sliced into rings
12 chicken livers, cut into strips
250 ml/8 fl oz cream
2 hard-boiled eggs, chopped
10 ml/2 teaspoons paprika
hot cooked rice

1. Melt half the butter in a frying pan. Add the onions and fry until golden brown. Remove the onions from the pan using a slotted spoon.

2. Add the chicken liver to the pan and fry for 5 minutes, stirring frequently. Remove the liver from the pan with a slotted spoon.

3. Add the remaining butter to the pan and melt it. Stir in the cream, eggs, paprika, and salt and pepper to taste. Return the liver and onions to the pan and mix into the sauce. Cook gently for 5 minutes.

4. Serve hot, with rice.

Serves 4

Chicken Maryland

25 g/1 oz flour
15 ml/1 tablespoon grated lemon rind
2 × 1 kg/2 lb chickens, halved
2 eggs, beaten
75 g/3 oz fresh breadcrumbs
oil for deep frying
50 g/2 oz butter
4 bananas, peeled and sliced lengthways
Corn fritters
125 g/4 oz flour
1 egg
175 ml/6 fl oz milk
225 g/8 oz sweetcorn kernels

1. Put the flour, lemon rind, and salt and pepper into a polythene bag. Add the chicken pieces and shake to coat them on all sides. Dip the chicken pieces in the beaten eggs, then coat with breadcrumbs. Repeat the egg-and-crumbing process, then chill the chicken for 2 hours.

2. Meanwhile, for the corn fritters, sift the flour and a little salt into a mixing bowl. Add the egg and milk and beat to make a smooth batter. Stir in the corn.

3. Heat oil in a deep fat fryer to 180°C/350°F. Deep fry the chicken pieces, two at a time, for 15–20 minutes. Drain on paper towels.

4. Increase the heat of the oil to 190°C/375°F. Drop heaped tablespoons of the corn batter into the oil and fry for 3 minutes or until puffed up and golden. Drain on paper towels and keep hot.

5. Melt the butter in a frying pan. Add the bananas and fry for about 3 minutes or until golden brown on both sides. Serve the chicken with the fritters and fried bananas.

Serves 4

Chicken Tetrazzini

175 g/6 oz vermicelli
65 g/2½ oz butter
30 ml/2 tablespoons flour
450 ml/¾ pint chicken stock
grated nutmeg
250 ml/8 fl oz double cream
45 ml/3 tablespoons pale dry sherry or white wine
700 g/1½ lb shredded cooked chicken meat
225 g/½ lb mushrooms, sliced
50 g/2 oz Parmesan cheese, grated

1. Preheat the grill. Cook the vermicelli in boiling water until it is tender. Drain and set aside.

2. Meanwhile, melt 50 g/1½ oz of the butter in a saucepan. Stir in the flour and cook for 3 minutes. Gradually stir in the stock. Bring to the boil, stirring, and simmer until thickened and smooth. Season with salt, pepper, and nutmeg. Stir in the cream, sherry or wine and chicken. Remove from the heat and keep hot.

3. Melt the remaining butter in a frying pan. Add the mushrooms and fry briskly until just tender.

4. Spread the vermicelli in a buttered flameproof dish. Scatter over the mushrooms. Pour the chicken mixture over the top.

5. Sprinkle with the cheese and grill just long enough to brown the top. Serve bubbling hot.

Serves 4

Chicken à la King

25 g/1 oz butter
1 green pepper, cored, seeded and finely chopped
175 g/6 oz thinly sliced mushrooms
15 ml/1 tablespoon flour
5 ml/1 teaspoon salt
350 ml/12 fl oz milk
250 ml/8 fl oz cream
700 g/1½ lb diced cooked chicken meat
3 egg yolks
10 ml/2 teaspoons lemon juice
15 ml/1 tablespoon paprika
10 ml/2 teaspoons chopped parsley
45 ml/3 tablespoons sweet sherry

1. Melt the butter in a saucepan. Add the green pepper and fry for 5 minutes. Add the mushrooms and continue frying for 3 minutes.

2. Stir in the flour and salt and cook for 2 minutes. Gradually stir in the milk and cream. Bring to the boil, stirring. Add the chicken and mix well. Cook very gently for 5 minutes.

3. Lightly beat the egg yolks with the lemon juice, paprika, parsley and sherry. Add about 60 ml/4 tablespoons of the hot sauce from the pan, then stir this mixture into the remaining sauce. Continue cooking very gently for about 4 minutes. Do not let the mixture boil. Serve hot, with rice.

Serves 4

Brunswick Stew

65 g/2½ oz butter
8 chicken pieces
1 large onion, sliced
1 green pepper, cored, seeded and chopped
300 ml/½ pint chicken stock
450 g/1 lb canned tomatoes, drained
2.5 ml/½ teaspoon cayenne pepper
15 ml/1 tablespoon Worcestershire sauce
2.5 ml/½ teaspoon salt
225 g/8 oz canned sweetcorn kernels
450 g/1 lb canned butter beans
15 ml/1 tablespoon flour

1. Melt 50 g/2 oz of the butter in a large saucepan. Add the chicken pieces and brown on all sides. Remove the chicken from the pan.

2. Add the onion and green pepper to the pan and fry until the onion is softened. Stir in the stock, tomatoes, cayenne pepper, Worcestershire sauce and salt and bring to the boil. Return the chicken pieces to the pan. Cover and simmer for 40 minutes.

3. Stir in the sweetcorn and butter beans and continue simmering, covered, for 15 minutes.

4. Mix the remaining butter with the flour to make a paste. Add to the stew in small pieces and stir until thickened. Taste and adjust the seasoning before serving.

Serves 4–6

VEGETABLES & SALADS

Succotash

---

4 bacon rashers, rinded
350 g/12 oz canned sweetcorn
350 g/12 oz canned butter beans
75 ml/3 fl oz cream

1. Fry the bacon in a saucepan until it has rendered its fat and is crisp. Drain on paper towels. Crumble and reserve.

2. Pour off all but about 20 ml/1½ tablespoons of the bacon fat from the pan. Add the sweetcorn and butter beans and heat through gently, stirring.

3. Stir in the cream, crumbled bacon, and salt and pepper to taste. Cook gently for a further 3 minutes or until piping hot.

Serves 4

Harvard Beets

450 g/1 lb beetroot
50 g/2 oz sugar
5 ml/1 teaspoon cornflour
50 ml/2 fl oz vinegar
125 ml/4 fl oz water

1. Put the beetroots into a saucepan and cover with water. Bring to the boil, cover and simmer for 50 minutes–1¼ hours, depending on the size of the beetroots. Drain and, when cool enough to handle, peel and slice.

2. Mix together the sugar and cornflour. Put the vinegar and water in a saucepan and heat until lukewarm. Stir in the sugar mixture and bring to the boil, stirring. Simmer for 2 minutes or until smooth and thick.

3. Add the beetroot to the pan and baste well with the sauce. Cook gently for 5 minutes or until the beetroot is heated through. Serve hot.

Serves 4

Boston Baked Beans

1 kg/2 lb dried haricot or kidney beans
10 ml/2 teaspoons salt
1 large onion, chopped
225 g/½ lb salt pork, thickly sliced
75 g/3 oz brown sugar
75 ml/5 tablespoons molasses
15 ml/1 tablespoon mustard powder
5 ml/1 teaspoon pepper

1. Put the beans in a saucepan and cover with cold water. Add half the salt. Bring to the boil, then half-cover the pan and simmer for 30 minutes.

2. Preheat the oven to 130°C/250°F (Gas ½). Drain the beans. Put the onion in the bottom of a casserole. Add a layer of beans, then cover with half the salt pork slices. Add the remaining beans and salt pork.

3. Mix together the sugar, molasses, mustard, pepper, and remaining salt. Pour into the casserole and add enough boiling water to cover the mixture.

4. Cover and bake for 5 hours, adding more boiling water from time to time so that the beans are kept covered.

5. Take off the lid and continue baking for 45 minutes or until a crust has formed on top. Serve hot.

Serves 6–8

Chef's Salad

1 lettuce, shredded
125 g/4 oz cooked chicken meat, cut into strips
125 g/4 oz cooked ham, cut into strips
125 g/4 oz Gruyère cheese, cut into strips
2 hard-boiled eggs, thinly sliced
15 ml/1 tablespoon finely chopped onion

1. Put the lettuce into a large salad bowl. Arrange the chicken, ham, cheese, and eggs on top and scatter over the onion.

2. Serve with your favourite dressing, such as French, Thousand Island or Blue Cheese (see page 40)

Serves 4

Caesar Salad

175 ml/6 fl oz olive oil
4 slices of white bread, crusts removed and cut into small cubes
1 garlic clove, halved
30 ml/2 tablespoons wine vinegar
5 ml/1 teaspoon lemon juice
2.5 ml/½ teaspoon Worcestershire sauce
1.25 ml/¼ teaspoon mustard powder
1.25 ml/¼ teaspoon sugar
1 egg
2 Cos lettuces, torn into pieces
6 anchovy fillets, chopped
50 g/2 oz Parmesan cheese, grated

1. Heat 50 ml/2 fl oz of the oil in a frying pan. Add the bread cubes and fry until golden brown on all sides. Drain these croûtons on paper towels.

2. Rub the cut surfaces of the garlic clove over the base and sides of a salad bowl. Discard the garlic.

3. Put the vinegar, lemon juice, Worcestershire sauce, mustard, sugar, the remaining oil, and salt and pepper to taste into the bowl. Mix well together.

4. Put the egg into a saucepan of boiling water and cook for 1 minute.

5. Meanwhile, add the lettuce to the salad bowl and toss to coat with the dressing. Scatter the anchovies, cheese and croûtons over the lettuce.

6. Break the egg on top. Toss the salad and serve immediately.

Serves 8

Blue Cheese Dressing

125 g/4 oz crumbled blue cheese
125 ml/4 fl oz mayonnaise
125 ml/4 fl oz double or soured cream

1. Beat the cheese into the mayonnaise, then beat in the cream.

2. Season to taste with salt and pepper and serve. Keep any leftover dressing in the refrigerator.

Makes about 300 ml/½ pint

Green Goddess Dressing

250 ml/8 fl oz mayonnaise
2 anchovy fillets, finely chopped
3 spring onions, finely chopped
30 ml/2 tablespoons chopped parsley
10 ml/2 teaspoons chopped fresh tarragon or 5 ml/1 teaspoon dried tarragon
15 ml/1 tablespoon tarragon vinegar
175 ml/6 fl oz soured cream

1. Mix together the mayonnaise, anchovies, spring onions, parsley, tarragon, vinegar, and pepper to taste.

2. Fold in the soured cream and chill for 30 minutes before serving. Keep any leftover dressing in the refrigerator.

Makes about 350 ml/12 fl oz

Mayonnaise, the basic ingredient in both Blue Cheese Dressing and Green Goddess Dressing.

DESSERTS

Maple Walnut Ice Cream

250 ml/8 fl oz maple syrup
3 eggs, separated
1.25 ml/¼ teaspoon salt
5 ml/1 teaspoon vanilla flavouring
250 ml/8 fl oz double cream
50 g/2 oz chopped walnuts

1. Put the maple syrup in the top of a double saucepan. Heat but do not let it boil.

2. Stir 30 ml/2 tablespoons of the warm syrup into the egg yolks, then add this mixture to the remaining syrup in the pan. Cook gently, stirring, until the mixture thickens.

3. Stir in the salt and vanilla and remove from the heat. Cool, then chill for 1 hour.

4. Whip the cream until thick and fold into the maple syrup mixture. Whisk the egg whites until stiff and fold in.

5. Remove the dividers from an ice cube tray and pour in the maple syrup mixture. Freeze for about 1 hour or until the mixture is frozen around the edges.

6. Tip the partially frozen mixture into a bowl and beat well. Stir in the nuts. Return the mixture to the ice cube tray and freeze for a further 3 hours.

Serves 4

Knickerbocker Glory

225 g/½ lb strawberries, hulled and halved
4 scoops of vanilla ice cream
4 ripe peaches, peeled, stoned and sliced
4 scoops of chocolate ice cream
50 g/2 oz plain chocolate
45 ml/3 tablespoons brandy
175 ml/6 fl oz whipping cream
4 maraschino cherries

1. Divide the strawberries between four sundae glasses. Top each with a scoop of vanilla ice cream.

2. Divide the peach slices between the glasses and top with a scoop of chocolate ice cream.

3. Melt the chocolate gently with the brandy. Pour this sauce over the chocolate ice cream

4. Whip the cream until thick and pipe or spoon it over the chocolate sauce.

5. Top each sundae with a cherry and serve.

Serves 4

Cherries Jubilee

450 g/1 lb canned black cherries, stoned
1.25 ml/¼ teaspoon ground cinnamon
15 ml/1 tablespoon sugar
10 ml/2 teaspoons arrowroot
50 ml/2 fl oz brandy
vanilla ice cream

1. Drain the cherries, reserving 250 ml/8 fl oz of the syrup.

2. Put the syrup in a saucepan and add the cinnamon, sugar and arrowroot. Bring to the boil, stirring, and simmer until smooth and thickened.

3. Add the cherries and simmer for a further 2–3 minutes to heat them through.

4. Warm the brandy and add to the cherry mixture. Pour over vanilla ice cream and set alight. Serve flaming.

Serves 6

Strawberry Shortbread Cake

225 g/8 oz flour
50 g/2 oz icing sugar
175 g/6 oz butter
1 egg yolk
350 ml/2 fl oz double cream
450 g/1 lb strawberries, hulled
30 ml/2 tablespoons caster sugar

1. Sift the flour and icing sugar into a mixing bowl. Add the butter and cut into small pieces. Knead to make a smooth dough, adding the egg yolk and at least 30 ml/2 tablespoons of the cream. Chill for 30 minutes.

2. Preheat the oven to 190°C/375°F (Gas 5). Divide the dough in half and roll out each piece to a 23 cm/9 in round. Place the rounds on well-greased baking sheets. Mark one of the rounds into eight wedges. Bake for 12–15 minutes or until the edges of the shortbreads are golden brown. Cool.

3. Slice the strawberries. Whip the remaining cream until thick and fold in the strawberries.

4. Place the unmarked shortbread round on a serving plate and pile the strawberry and cream mixture on top.

5. Break the second shortbread round into the marked wedges and arrange these over the cream filling. Sprinkle over the caster sugar and serve.

Serves 8

Shoofly Pie

shortcrust pastry made with 175 g/6 oz flour
175 g/6 oz flour
125 g/4 oz butter
225 g/8 oz brown sugar
5 ml/1 teaspoon bicarbonate of soda
250 ml/8 fl oz boiling water
175 ml/6 fl oz molasses
175 ml/6 fl oz clear honey

1. Preheat the oven to 190°C/375°F (Gas 5). Roll out the dough and use to line a 23 cm/9 in pie dish or flan ring.

2. Sift the flour into a mixing bowl. Rub in the butter until the mixture resembles breadcrumbs. Stir in the sugar.

3. Dissolve the bicarbonate of soda in the water, then stir in the molasses and honey. Pour the mixture into the pastry case. Sprinkle the flour and butter mixture over the top.

4. Bake for 10 minutes, then reduce the oven temperature to 180°C/350°F (Gas 4). Continue baking for 25–30 minutes. Cool before serving.

Serves 4–6

Pecan Pie

shortcrust pastry made with 175 g/6 oz flour
50 g/2 oz pecans
3 eggs
250 ml/8 oz golden syrup
75 g/3 oz brown sugar
2.5 ml/½ teaspoon vanilla flavouring
1.25 ml/¼ teaspoon salt

1. Preheat the oven to 220°C/425°F (Gas 7). Roll out the dough and use to line a 23 cm/9 in pie dish or flan ring. Bake blind for 20 minutes or until golden brown and firm. Remove from the oven and cool slightly.

2. Arrange the pecans in the base of the pastry case in concentric circles.

3. Beat the eggs with the syrup, sugar, vanilla and salt. Pour over the pecans in the pastry case, being careful not to disturb their pattern. They will rise to the surface.

4. Bake for 10 minutes, then reduce the oven temperature to 180°C/350°F (Gas 4). Continue baking for 30 minutes. Cool before serving.

Serves 4–6

Coconut Cream Pie

shortcrust pastry made with 175 g/6 oz flour
225 g/8 oz sugar
65 g/2½ oz flour
750 ml/1¼ pints lukewarm milk
3 egg yolks
25 g/1 oz butter
5 ml/1 teaspoon vanilla flavouring
50 g/2 oz desiccated coconut

1. Preheat the oven to 220°C/425°F (Gas 7). Roll out the dough and use to line a 23 cm/9 in pie dish or flan ring. Bake blind for 20 minutes or until golden brown and firm. Remove from the oven and cool slightly.

2. Put the sugar and flour in a saucepan and gradually stir in the milk. Cook, stirring, for 10 minutes or until thickened. Cool slightly.

3. Beat the egg yolks with 45 ml/3 tablespoons of the milk mixture. Stir this into the remaining mixture in the pan. Return to the heat and cook gently, stirring, until the mixture is very thick. Stir in the butter, vanilla, and all but 30 ml/2 tablespoons of the coconut.

4. Pour the coconut mixture into the pastry case and sprinkle the reserved coconut on top.

5. Bake for 15 minutes. Cool before serving.

Serves 8

Chocolate Chiffon Pie

125 g/4 oz Brazil nuts
25 g/1 oz sugar
Filling
15 g/½ oz gelatine
125 g/4 oz sugar
1.25 ml/¼ teaspoon salt
250 ml/8 fl oz milk
2 eggs, separated
225 g/8 oz plain chocolate, broken into pieces
5 ml/1 teaspoon vanilla flavouring
350 ml/12 fl oz whipping cream
30 ml/2 tablespoons chopped Brazil nuts

1. Preheat the oven to 200°C/400°F (Gas 6). Grind the nuts in a food mill or blender. Mix with the sugar, then press over the base and sides of a 23 cm/9 in pie dish or flan ring. Bake the nut crust for 8–10 minutes or until lightly browned. Cool.

2. For the filling, put the gelatine, half the sugar, and the salt in the top of a double saucepan. Stir in the milk, egg yolks, and chocolate. Cook, stirring, until the gelatine has dissolved and the chocolate has melted. Remove from the heat and stir in the vanilla. Cool the chocolate mixture, then chill until it is on the point of setting.

3. Whip the cream until thick. Fold about two-thirds of the cream into the chocolate mixture. Whisk the egg whites until stiff. Add the remaining sugar and whisk for a further 1 minute. Fold the egg whites into the chocolate mixture. Pour the filling into the nut crust. Chill for 3 hours or until set.

4. Decorate with the remaining whipped cream and the chopped Brazil nuts.

Serves 6–8

Angel Cake

75 g/3 oz flour
15 ml/1 tablespoon cornflour
2.5 ml/½ teaspoon ground cinnamon
225 g/8 oz sugar
10 egg whites
15 ml/1 tablespoon lemon juice
15 ml/1 tablespoon hot water
5 ml/1 teaspoon cream of tartar
grated rind of 2 oranges
225 g/½ lb strawberries, hulled
icing sugar

1. Preheat the oven to 180°C/350°F (Gas 4). Sift the flour, cornflour, a little salt, and cinnamon into a mixing bowl. Add about one-third of the sugar. Sift these ingredients twice more.

2. Divide the egg whites, lemon juice, and hot water between two large mixing bowls. Whisk the contents of one bowl until foamy, then add half the cream of tartar and continue whisking until the mixture will stand in stiff peaks. Whisk the contents of the second bowl in the same way, adding the remaining cream of tartar. Tip into the first mixture.

3. Sift in the remaining sugar and the orange rind and beat for 1 minute. Gently fold in the flour mixture. Spoon into a 22 cm/8½ in angel cake or ring tin that is 10 cm/4 in deep. Bake for 45 minutes or until the cake will spring back when lightly pressed.

4. Remove the cake from the oven and invert it over a bottle or some other tall object. Cool completely.

5. Remove the cake from the tin and place it on a serving plate. Fill the centre with the strawberries and sprinkle with icing sugar.

Serves 8

Devil's Food Cake

125 g/4 oz plain chocolate
250 ml/8 fl oz milk
175 g/6 oz brown sugar
1 egg yolk
2 eggs, separated
275 g/10 oz flour
1.25 ml/¼ teaspoon salt
5 ml/1 teaspoon bicarbonate of soda
125 g/ 4 oz butter
175 g/6 oz caster sugar
50 ml/2 fl oz water
5 ml/1 teaspoon vanilla flavouring
1 packet American fudge frosting mix

1. Preheat the oven to 180°C/350°F (Gas 4). Put the chocolate, milk, sugar and 1 egg yolk in the top of a double saucepan. Cook, stirring, until the chocolate melts and thickens slightly. Remove from the heat.

2. Sift the flour, salt and bicarbonate of soda into a mixing bowl. In another bowl, cream the butter with the caster sugar until the mixture is light and fluffy. Beat in the remaining egg yolks, then add the flour and water and mix to make a smooth batter. Stir in the vanilla and the chocolate mixture.

3. Beat the egg whites until stiff and fold them into the mixture. Divide the mixture between three greased and floured 20.5 cm/8 in sandwich cake tins. Bake for 25 minutes or until a skewer inserted into the centre of each cake comes out clean. Cool on a wire rack.

4. Make the frosting according to packet instructions. Sandwich the cake layers together with about three-quarters of the frosting. Use the remainder to cover the top and sides of the cake, swirling it into a decorative pattern.

Serves 8

BREADS & COOKIES

San Francisco Sourdough Bread

1.5 kg/3 lb strong white flour
30 ml/2 tablespoons sugar
20 ml/1½ tablespoons salt
900 ml/1½ pints water
30 ml/2 tablespoons oil
Starter
225 g/8 oz strong white flour
125 g/4 oz sugar
450 ml/¾ pint milk

1. First make the starter. Put all the ingredients into a screw-top jar and shake to form a smooth paste. Leave, covered, in a warm place for 1 week.

2. Sift the flour, sugar, and salt into a bowl. Add the starter, water and oil and mix to make a dough. Tip the dough on to a floured surface and knead for about 5 minutes or until the dough is smooth and elastic. Shape into a ball and place in a greased polythene bag. Leave to rise for 2 hours.

3. Preheat the oven to 190°C/375°F (Gas 5). Punch down the dough and knead it for a further 10 minutes. Divide it in half and shape each piece into a round, about 15 cm/6 in in diameter.

4. Put the rounds on greased baking sheets. Cut a deep cross in the top of each round. Bake for 1–1½ hours: it should sound hollow like a drum. Cool on a wire rack.

Makes 2 loaves

Parker House Rolls

---

15 g/½ oz dry yeast
75 g/3 oz sugar
10 ml/2 teaspoons lukewarm water
350 ml/12 fl oz milk
140 g/4½ oz butter
700 g/1½ lb flour
5 ml/1 teaspoon salt
1 egg, beaten

1. Mix the yeast with 2.5 ml/½ teaspoon of the sugar and the water. Leave in a warm place until the mixture is frothy. Scald the milk in a saucepan. Remove from the heat and add 75 g/3 oz of the butter. Stir until the butter has melted, then leave the mixture to cool to lukewarm.

2. Sift the flour, salt and remaining sugar into a mixing bowl. Add the yeast and milk mixtures and the egg and mix to a dough. Tip the dough on to a floured surface and knead for 10 minutes or until smooth and elastic. Shape the dough into a ball and place it in a greased polythene bag. Leave to rise for 2 hours.

3. Punch down the dough and knead it for a further 3 minutes. Roll it out to about 1 cm/½ in thick. Spread 25 g/1 oz of the remaining butter over the dough, then cut it into 7.5 cm/3 in rounds. Make a shallow cut in the centre of each round and fold into semi-circles, pressing the edges together to seal.

4. Place the rolls on greased baking sheets, spacing them well apart. Melt the remaining butter and brush it over the rolls. Cover and let rise for 45 minutes.

5. Preheat the oven to 240°C/475°F (Gas 9). Bake the rolls for 15–20 minutes or until golden brown.

Makes about 40

Spoon Bread

150 g/5 oz maize flour
5 ml/1 teaspoon baking powder
1.25 ml/¼ teaspoon bicarbonate of soda
2.5 ml/½ teaspoon salt
3 eggs, beaten
450 ml/¾ pint buttermilk
25 g/1 oz butter

1. Preheat the oven to 200°C/400°F (Gas 6). Sift the maize flour, baking powder, bicarbonate of soda and salt into a mixing bowl. Add the eggs and mix well, then gradually beat in the buttermilk to make a smooth batter.

2. Put the butter in a 20.5 × 20.5 × 5 cm/8 × 8 × 2 in baking tin or a 1.3 litre/2¼ pint capacity soufflé dish. Warm in the oven until the butter has melted.

3. Remove the tin or dish from the oven and tilt it to coat the base and sides with melted butter. Pour any excess butter into the maize flour and stir it in, then pour the mixture into the tin or dish.

4. Bake for 35 minutes and serve hot.

Serves 4

Blueberry Muffins

400 g/14 oz flour
7.5 ml/1½ teaspoons salt
175 g/6 oz sugar
20 ml/4 teaspoons baking powder
4 eggs
125 g/4 oz butter, melted
300 ml/½ pint milk
275 g/10 oz blueberries or bilberries

1. Preheat the oven to 230°C/450°F (Gas 8). Sift the flour, salt, sugar and baking powder into a mixing bowl.

2. In another bowl, beat the eggs until they are pale and thick. Beat in the melted butter and milk followed by the flour mixture. Do not overbeat: the ingredients should be just combined.

3. Coat the blueberries or bilberries lightly in a little extra flour (this prevents them sinking to the bottom of the muffins), then fold them into the batter.

4. Divide the batter between 36 greased and floured muffin pans. Bake for 15 minutes or until risen and golden brown. Serve hot.

Makes 36

Brownies

175 g/6 oz plain chocolate
30 ml/2 tablespoons water
125 g/4 oz butter
125 g/4 oz sugar
5 ml/1 teaspoon vanilla flavouring
125 g/4 oz self-raising flour
2 eggs
50 g/2 oz chopped walnuts

1. Preheat the oven to 170°C/325°F (Gas 3). Put the chocolate, water and butter in a saucepan and heat gently, stirring until the mixture is smooth. Remove from the heat and stir in the sugar and vanilla. Cool slightly.

2. Sift the flour and a pinch of salt into a mixing bowl. Add the eggs and chocolate mixture and beat until smooth. Fold in the walnuts.

3. Pour into a greased 20.5 cm/8 in square baking tin. Bake for 30–35 minutes or until a skewer inserted into the centre comes out clean.

4. Cool in the tin, then cut into squares to serve.

Makes about 16

(Top) Brownies
(Bottom) Chocolate Chip Cookies

Chocolate Chip Cookies

125 g/4 oz butter
125 g/4 oz granulated sugar
75 g/3 oz brown sugar
1 egg
2.5 ml/½ teaspoon vanilla flavouring
175 g/6 oz flour
2.5 ml/½ teaspoon salt
2.5 ml/¼ teaspoon bicarbonate of soda
50 g/2 oz chopped walnuts
50 g/2 oz chocolate chips

1. Preheat the oven to 190°C/375°F (Gas 5). Cream the butter with the sugars until the mixture is light and fluffy. Beat in the egg and vanilla.

2. Sift the flour with the salt and bicarbonate of soda, then add to the butter mixture. Beat until smooth. Mix in the walnuts and chocolate chips.

3. Drop teaspoons of the mixture on to greased baking sheets, spacing them well apart to allow for spreading. Bake for 10–15 minutes or until the cookies are golden brown. Cool on a wire rack.

Makes about 30

Pretzels

15 g/½ oz dry yeast
2.5 ml/½ teaspoon sugar
250 ml/8 fl oz lukewarm milk
25 g/1 oz butter
350 g/12 oz flour
2.5 ml/½ teaspoon salt
15 ml/1 tablespoon caraway seeds
1 egg, beaten

1. Mix the yeast with the sugar and 30 ml/2 tablespoons of the milk. Leave in a warm place until frothy. Scald the remaining milk in a pan. Remove from the heat and add the butter. Stir until the butter has melted, then leave to cool to lukewarm.

2. Sift the flour and salt into a mixing bowl. Add 10 ml/2 teaspoons of the caraway seeds and the yeast and milk mixtures. Mix to a dough. Tip on to a floured surface and knead for 10 minutes or until smooth and elastic. Shape into a ball and place it in a greased polythene bag. Leave to rise for 45 minutes.

3. Punch down the dough and knead for a further 3 minutes. Roll into a sausage about 30.5 cm/12 in long. Cut the roll into 48 pieces. Roll each piece into a thin sausage about 15 cm/6 in long. Put on a flat surface and curve the ends towards you. Cross the loop halfway along each side and twist once. Bend the ends back and press firmly on to the curve of the loop.

4. Preheat the oven to 190°C/375°F (Gas 5). Drop the pretzels, a few at a time, into a pan of boiling water and cook until they rise to the surface. Remove and drain on paper towels. When all the pretzels have been 'boiled', arrange them on greased baking sheets.

5. Coat with beaten egg and the remaining caraway. Bake for 15 minutes or until golden brown. Cool on wire racks.

Makes 48

INDEX